The exhibition and the catalogue were very kindly supported by:
ALCAN, ALUKÖNIGSTAHL, BS Modelshop Vienna, DuPont CORIAN, Fischer-Parkett, FUNDERMAX, ING Real Estate, GIRA, KALLCO,
NEUES LEBEN, ROCKWOOL Österreich, vitra., Wien-Süd, MISCHEK -Wiener Heim, wohnfonds_wien
With special thanks to ZUMTOBEL for the generous support.

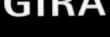

DELUGAN MEISSL ASSOCIATED ARCHITECTS
inTENSE repose

AEDES   ZUMTOBEL

RAUMSHIFT-LABOR

Segelt das Team von Delugan Meissl Associated Architects ihr Gedanken-, Form- und Wertelabor in zunehmender flux-Geschwindigkeit durch die Stadträume, entsteht, getrieben von einer dynamischen nicht weniger methodischen Auseinandersetzung, eine Art „Raum-Zeit-Schmelze".

Eben dies ist der Kulminations-Moment, in dem es ihnen gelingt, für einen präzisen Ort mit den Anforderungen und Funktionsvorgaben des Bauherren, unter Einbeziehung der stadt-räumlichen Umgebung und den für sie immerfort neu zu definierenden Einflüssen aus dem „Zeitfenster der Gegenwart" in der ihnen eigenen Ästhetik ein Meisterwerk entstehen zu lassen.

So atemzehrend dieser Satz, so überwältigend die von den Architekten geschaffenen Raumwelten. Aussen wie innen eindeutigen Funktionen zugeordnet, werden sie dennoch entgrenzt, gegeneinander verschoben, so dass man als Benutzer und Betrachter in diesem Spannungsfeld geradewegs zu schweben beginnt. Durchaus nicht schwerelos. Eigentümer wie Benutzer der von Delugan Meissl entworfenen Architekturen können sich verorten. Die Großzügigkeit der geschaffenen Räume – für Delugan Meissl ein wichtiges konzeptionelles Element, – erfahren in der jeweiligen persönlichen Aneignung individuelle Ausstrahlung und Kraft. Das österreichische Avantgarde Studio bringt dabei Gegensätze wie Geschwindigkeit und Verharren, Intimität und Weite, Exponiertheit und Geborgenheit in seinen Architekturen spannungsvoll zum Ausdruck.

Wir freuen uns auf den Diskurs, den Ausstellung und Katalog an den verschiedenen Orten und in der jeweiligen Gegenwart mit Sicherheit auslösen werden.

Kristin Feireiss, Hans-Jürgen Commerell

SPACESHIFT-LABORATORY

As the team of Delugan Meissl Associated Architects navigates their sailing laboratory of concepts, forms and values at an accelerating flux velocity through the urban realm, there emerges a "spatial-temporal fusion" that is propelled by dynamic and nonetheless methodical approach.

This is precisely the moment of culmination in which they succeed – at a definite location, in conformity with the requirements and functional prerequisites of the client, in a way that incorporates the urban environment and responds to a set of perpetually redefined influences – in allowing a masterwork to emerge from the "temporal window of the present," one that embodies their own singular aesthetic.

Long-breathed as this sentence might seem, it conveys something of the overwhelming quality of the spatial worlds created by these architects. Dedicated on the outside as well as within to unambiguous functions, inside and outside are at the same time deprived of distinct delimitations and shifted one into the another, so that beholders and users almost begin to float within a field of tension. But not at all the weightlessly. Owners and users of architecture designed by Delugan Meissl are always able to locate themselves in space. Depending upon an individual's personal mode of appropriation, the sheer generosity of their spaces – a crucial conceptual elements for Delugan Meissl – can be experienced in all their highly individualized vibrancy and power. In their architecture, this Austrian avant-garde studio brings contraries such as velocity and persistence, intimacy and expansion, exposedness and concealment, into a highly tensed expressiveness.

We are looking forward to the discussion this exhibition and catalog are bound to ignite at its various locations and contrasting temporalities.

DELUGAN MEISSL ASSOCIATED ARCHITECTS inTENSE repose

Delugan Meissl Associated Architects begreifen Raum nicht a priori als statisch, sondern in erster Linie als dynamische und variable INTERAKTION von Mensch und Umgebung. Der Raum wird im Sinne verschiedener GESCHWINDIGKEITEN interpretiert: Die Architektur impliziert das Moment der Beweglichkeit als Körperbewegung in spannungsvoller Ruhe und initiiert zugleich das sinnliche Nachvollziehen dieser Bewegungsabläufe durch den Menschen.

Wie kann sich BEWEGUNG über die Form und den Inhalt, wie über das unmittelbare Erleben ausdrücken? Scheinbare Gegensätzlichkeiten wie Geschwindigkeit und Verharren, Intimität und Weite oder Geborgenheit und Exponiertheit werden in einen FLIESSENDEN RAUMGREIFENDEN ZUSAMMENHANG gestellt und mittels differenziert offener Wegesysteme verknüpft.

Die Strategie der programmatischen Abgrenzung wird zugunsten einer variablen Organisation der Unterschiede, der durchlässigen, differenzierten oder erweiterbaren GRENZE aufgehoben. In gleichem Maße wird die strikte Trennung von innen und außen unterlaufen – die Haut wird zum Raum und auf diese Weise besetzt und nutzbar.

Gebäude werden nicht als bloße Hülle verstanden, die im Nachhinein gefüllt und deren innewohnende Bewegung durch klassische Raumaufteilungen blockiert ist. Vielmehr erzeugt eine plastische Ausformulierung der AUSSENHAUT im Innenraum unterschiedliche räumliche Wertigkeiten, die sich aus dem FORMENVERLAUF der gesamten Architektur heraus entwickeln.

Es gilt grundsätzlich auszuloten, inwieweit Architektur die Fähigkeit besitzt, über ihr gewohntes Erscheinungsbild hinaus zu expandieren. Dies kann sich sowohl auf das Überschreiten klassischer Raumbegrenzungen und deren normierter Gestalt beziehen, als auch auf das Vermögen der Architektur, den Menschen dazu herauszufordern über den bloßen Gebrauch hinaus mit seiner Umgebung in ganzheitlich sinnlich erfahrbare Interaktion zu treten.

Delugan Meissl Associated Architects do not see space – a priori – as static, but rather as dynamic and variable INTERACTION between people and their environment. The interpretation of space is one of differing VELOCITIES. Architecture implies the moment of mobility – a body movement in tense repose –, initiating at the same time people's comprehension of these movements with all their senses.

How can MOVEMENT express itself through form and content, by direct experience? Apparent dichotomies such as speed and persistence, intimacy and expanse, or security and exposure are brought into a FLOWING SPATIAL CONTEXT and are linked through differentiated open PATHS.

The strategy of programmatic delimitation is abolished in favour of a variable organisation of differences, the permeable, intricately distinct, or extendable BORDER. To the same degree, the strict separation between the interior and exterior becomes subverted – the skin transforms into space and is rendered usable.

Buildings are not regarded as mere skins that are to be filled afterwards and whose intrinsic flow is blocked through the classical separation into rooms. Instead, they use a sculptural formulation of the EXTERIOR SKIN to produce different spatial valences on the inside, which arise out of the formal FLUX of the overall architecture.

The objective is to fathom the extent to which architecture possesses the potential of expanding beyond its familiar image. Both in terms of going beyond classical spatial limitations and their standardised guise, as well as of the capacity of architecture to challenge us to transcend mere utility and connect with our surroundings in an interaction that can be experienced holistically and sensorially.

LICHT UND ARCHITEKTUR

LIGHT AND ARCHITECTURE

Ohne Licht kein Raum – so kurz und präzise lässt sich eine weitreichende Erkenntnis formulieren, die die Beziehung zwischen einem Architekten und einem Lichtlösungsanbieter definiert. Sich mit Licht, und Architektur auseinander zu setzen, ist für Zumtobel seit Jahren Profession und spannende Herausforderung zugleich. Wir entwickeln zukunftsweisende Lichtlösungen, die bestmögliche Lichtqualität für den Menschen und die Schonung der natürlichen Ressourcen in eine ausgewogene Balance bringen. Das richtige Licht, seine geschickte Komposition und Lenkung machen Gebäude zu wahren Erlebniswelten. Denn Licht erfüllt nicht allein die Funktion. Licht ist vor allem ein emotionales Medium, das gezielt Stimmungen erzeugt, Botschaften transportiert, im Zusammenspiel mit Raum und Architektur ganz eigene Gestaltungskraft entfaltet.

Um als Lichtunternehmen wegweisend zu sein, muss man offen sein für die Suche nach noch nie da Gewesenem, nach Wandel und Erneuerung. Innovationskraft setzt also die Bereitschaft voraus, neue Wege zu gehen und Impulse aus dem Markt aufzunehmen. Zahlreiche solcher Innovationsimpulse für Produkte und Projektlösungen gehen von internationalen Partnerschaften aus. Im Mittelpunkt der gemeinsamen Arbeit steht die Entwicklung projektbezogener, individuell abgestimmter Lichtkonzeptionen. Was Licht im architektonischem Kontext alles leisten soll, erfahren wir erst durch den wechselseitigen Dialog mit jenen, die Licht anwenden, die Raum gestalten: den Architekten, Designern, Lichtplanern und auch Künstlern. Denn die beständige Auseinandersetzung mit ihren Visionen trägt dazu bei, unser Verständnis nachhaltig zu prägen, wie das Medium Licht als architektonische Erlebnisdimension verstanden und eingesetzt wird. Diese Partner bringen uns immer wieder an die Grenzen unserer eigenen Leistungsfähigkeit. Durch ihren Antrieb gelingt es uns, scheinbar Unmögliches letztendlich doch möglich zu machen.

Seit mehr als einem Jahrzehnt verbindet uns mit AedesBerlin eine fruchtbare „Kultur"-Partnerschaft durch die wir in unseren Lichtforen und -zentren bereits eine Reihe internationaler Beiträge präsentieren konnten um darüber mit Architekten, Designern, Künstlern, Stadtplanern und unsere Partnern sowie Mitarbeitern den Dialog kontinuierlich fortzusetzen, zu stimulieren und Anforderungen an zukünftige Bedürfnisse, Notwendigkeiten und Herausforderungen schon jetzt zu erarbeiten.

Mit großer Freude begleiten wir die Ausstellung inTENSE repose der Architektengemeinschaft Delugan Meissl, die sich in Ihrer Arbeit kontinuierlich an der Schnittstelle von Gegenwart und Zukunft bewegen und mit ihren Entwürfen die dynamische wie variable Interaktion von Mensch und Umgebung zum Thema machen. Mit dieser außergewöhnlichen Präsentation wie auch vielen weiteren aus den Bereichen Architektur, Kunst und Kultur bedanken wir uns bei unseren Partnern für das Vertrauen und die fruchtbare Zusammenarbeit und bringen unsere Verbundenheit zum Ausdruck.

No light, no space – bound in a nutshell in this formulation is a complex concept defining the relationship between an architect and a lighting solution supplier. Tackling the issues of light and architecture has for years been the profession and at the same time a dynamic challenge for Zumtobel. We develop trendsetting lighting solutions that bring optimum lighting quality for the individual into poised equilibrium with the protection and conservation of natural resources. The right light, its skilful composition and direction turn buildings into real worlds of experience. For light does not merely serve a functional purpose. Light is first and foremost an emotional medium, creating specific atmospheres, communicating messages, releasing a wholly individual, creative energy in the interplay of space and architecture.

To set new trends as a lighting company, you have to boldly embark on the quest for what has never been, for change, renewal, and innovation. Innovative power presumes the readiness to break new ground and wire up to new impulses from the market. Many such innovative impulses for products and project solutions are sourced from international partnerships. Collaboration concentrates on the development of project-related, individually adjusted lighting conceptions. We can only experience what light should achieve in an architectural context by a reciprocal dialogue with the people who use light, who design space: architects, designers, lighting designers, and last but not least artists – because the constant involvement with their visions has a share in profoundly forming our understanding of the medium of light and how it can be used as an architectural dimension of experience. Time and again, these partners bring us to the limits of our own capabilities. Their drive is what makes us eventually succeed in doing the impossible.

For more than a decade now, we have been associated with Aedes Berlin in a fruitful cultural partnership, through which we have been able to present a series of international contributions at our Light Centres, while at the same time engaging in continuous dialogue with architects, designers, artists, city planners and our partners, providing stimulus, while beginning today to come to terms with future requirements, necessities, and challenges.

We are delighted to assist with the exhibition inTENSE repose by the ambitious Viennese architectural association Delugan Meissl, whose works moves continuously along the interface between present and future, and whose designs explore the dynamic and variable interaction joining human individuals with their surroundings. With this extraordinary presentation, as with so many others from the realms of architecture, art and culture, we wish to thank our partners for their confidence and their fruitful collaboration, and to express our appreciation for the bonds existing between us.

Peter Matt
CEO Zumtobel

08.09

THE WORK OF DELUGAN MEISSL ASSOCIATED ARCHITECTS

This exhibition of projects by Delugan Meissl Associated Architects provides a welcome opportunity to reflect on the firm's body of work from the past decade and how it has changed and how it has remained constant. The range of projects on display includes two museums, a panoramic elevator, a city airport, and a number of housing projects, both individual and collective, thereby demonstrating the firm's adroitness in producing innovative solutions to problems of varying scales and programmatic issues.

Uniting all projects, however, is a consistent concern for the development of the building's skin. Rather than a two-dimensional membrane delineating the building's limit, in their work the skin is treated as an active zone serving as a filter of light and information. The skin becomes a thick, layered space mediating between inside and out, complicating their distinction. With each project, the firm also investigates new technologies for the skin's materiality, such as embedding the veneer with photovoltaic cells, or using Alucobond and Corian to sculpt supple surface formations in House Ray 1. Superficiality here becomes a virtue: the shallowness of "skin-deep beauty" is overcome by the profundity of deep skin beauty.

Delugan Meissl clearly draw from the language of modernism, adding to this an inspired use of materials to create new and innovative constructions that are at home in the contemporary city. The external form does not provide the most telling description of each project, as their design process focuses on the development of the building's section, and creating complex configurations of internal space. This is most evident in the firm's larger housing projects, such as City Lofts in Vienna, where an intricate system of interlocking levels creates modules of varying heights, allowing multiple dwelling types to be included within one building. Similarly, the HH Wienerberg building for subsidized housing uses modular systems and free facades to allow inhabitants to easily reconfigure the interior spaces.

These strategies for the skin work to complicate the relationship between inside and out. Techniques such as fragmentation and layering are used to create an abstract pattern on the external facades that only occasionally exposes the internal organization of the building. Ribbons of green landscape weave through the Wimbergergasse mixed-use development, tying the office spaces to a block of housing units. The layered façade of the housing block is composed of a framework of modular loggias and open spaces, extending the interior living spaces out to the edge of the building while simultaneously forcing a disrupted reading of those spaces from the outside. In the Amsterdam Filmmuseum, a reflective cladding is used so that the irregular, faceted building mirrors its physical surroundings while the interior spaces are obscured.

A close attention to skins does not preclude Delugan Meissl's capacity to work at the urban scale. In fact, the filtering achieved by a layering process on the façade also occurs at the level of the city. The 'Beam' at Donau-City is a horizontal high-rise that hovers above the ground on pilotis, creating an interstitial space beneath the building's mass. The building channels pedestrian flow transversely from one elongated facade to the other, allowing movement from the city fabric through to the edge of the Danube with which the long building is aligned. The Beam's horizontal form links it to the landscape, while its elevation creates a layering of space between the ground plane and the stacked levels of the housing block. Meaning in their work, thus, oscillates between the building's form and its surfaces.

Alexandra Quantrill and Terence Riley

10.11

POWERFUL AND SENSUAL

These are the words I would use to characterize the architecture of Delugan Meissl Associated Architects. Here is an architecture of generous gestures, sculptural but never gratuitously playful. On the contrary: it is extremely confident while at the same time inspiring confidence. At times, the buildings of Delugan Meissl seem to float or hover, yet are never suggestive of flight. They are always carefully positioned on the ground. Some of them seem to have grown out of the ground like old trees, ready to be climbed for a look out over the landscape, while others seem to have come to rest on the ground or on a base. This is not an architecture that plays variations on the clichés of weightlessness; it seems heavy and even extremely substantial. This is not an architecture that wants to deconstruct, but which instead takes construction and tectonics as self-evident parts of the experience of a new whole. Everything in these projects serves to celebrate the program and the surroundings. Yet, at the same time, the projects themselves almost breathe something like a new monumentality.

Bart Lootsma

1 STUDIO – 1 CRITIC

In 1993, Elke Delugan-Meissl and Roman Delugan established Delugan Meissl Architects in Vienna, a city with a particularly rich and multilayered contemporary architectural culture whose preoccupations run from a certain weakness for the playful and sickly sweet to a commitment to the most austere and acerbic design languages. It is a promiscuous range that has the effect of recalibrating the scale of design practice there, producing a certain cross-fertilization among positions that serves to transform the pursuit of technological logic with a much more vivid form of expression. Anywhere else, studios like Delugan Meissl Associated Architects would be doing things differently. But in Vienna, they are engaged in a hybrid form of architecture. (...)

The studio's work, which has concentrated so far on housing – mostly high-density and with a social agenda – is what might be called second-generation high-tech. The apartment block that they designed overlooking the Danube in Vienna's new Donau area has the transparency of all-glass walls and the structural frankness of Renzo Piano and Richard Rogers in their heyday. But the point here is not any residual belief in structural honesty but a kind of voyeuristic striptease. The eight-story block is hoisted up on pilotis to make the most of the views but also puts the residents in their south-facing all-glass-walled apartments on show. Privacy comes from tattooing the glass with barcode patterns. Delugan Meissl's version of high technology is a means to an end rather than a belief in technology for its own sake. In projects such as House Ray 1 in Vienna – in which interior and exterior are blurred by sculptural furniture that subverts the distinction between object and container – the partners demonstrate that their real interest is the creation of an edgy kind of space.

Deyan Sudjic
in: 10 x 10_2 100 Architects 10 Critics
PHAIDON PRESS LTD., London – New York, 2005

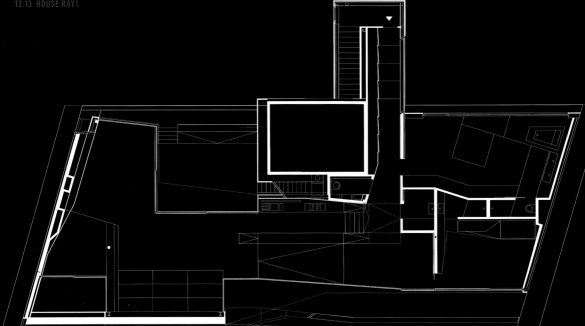

HOUSE RAY1 2003

Situated on the flat roof of a 1960s office building in the middle of the rooftop landscape of Vienna's fourth district, Ray 1 evolved out of the direct stimuli and spatial quality of the location. This origin, however, is by no means contradicted by the clash of the static mass and the dynamic form of architecture in motion; this juxtaposition rather serves to charge the structure.

The new building evolved out of the connection between the two buildings on either side, continuing the line of projection of the gables and providing, as it were, the missing link. The boundary between sky and earth, however, should not be taken as a dividing line separating the roof and the surrounding context, but as a permeable border zone that itself becomes a space for living.

Recesses and folds create transparent zones and sheltered terraced landscapes on both sides of the building, providing opportunities for experiencing the structure's open layout, from the entrance all the way up to the accessible roof area.

The outer skin, which is coated with Alucobond, defines the contours of the apartment's interior, suggesting varying valences for different zones and niches. The intention was to create a shell that would function as a programmable medium for furniture; one would be transformed through the architecture. The interior space is designed as a loft whose various functional areas are defined by different floor levels.

Floor area: 230 m²
Built-up area: 340 m²

Project: Rooftop Expansion
Location: Vienna
Client: Delugan Meissl

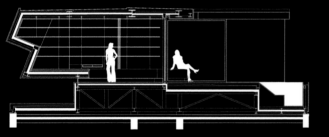

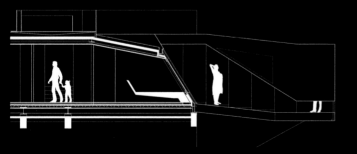

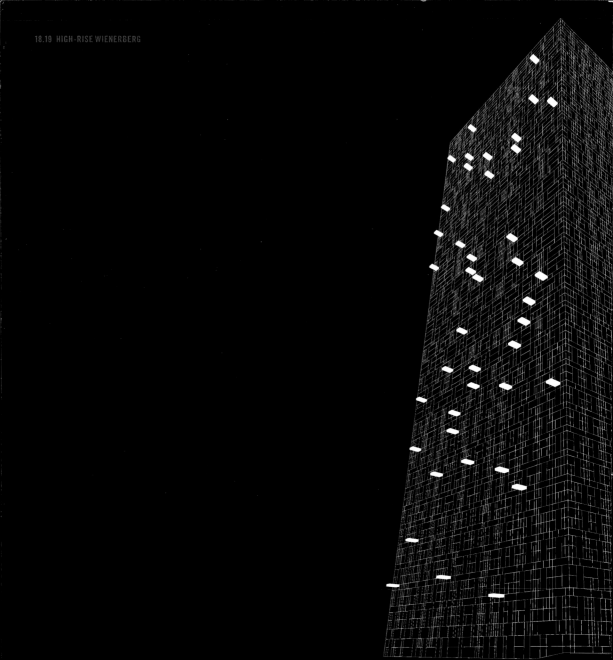

HIGH-RISE WIENERBERG 2005

The elegant silhouette of the tower is marked by two contrasting façade typologies, which have been determined by their respective orientations. On the south side, the living space is extended by a layer of loggias 1.8 meters deep, which, given the crowded surroundings of the Wienerberg neighborhood, provides a welcome private zone of free space whose outer glazed wall resembles a "delicate curtain."

By contrast, the northeast side appears introverted and closed. The effect of the dark monolithic impression of the Eternit cladding is heightened by its juxtaposition with freely arranged French windows and individual cantilevered shields.

The aim of this façade design is to avoid a stereotyped readability of recurring apartment types in the exterior appearance of the building, and based on the internal demands of the apartments, to bring together the internal heterogeneous structure in an overall graphically ordered outer skin.

Floor area: 16,600 m^2
Built-up area: 720 m^2
Number of apartments: 204
Height: 99 m

Project: Residential Building
Location: Vienna
Client: Daheim Wohnbau GmbH, Vienna

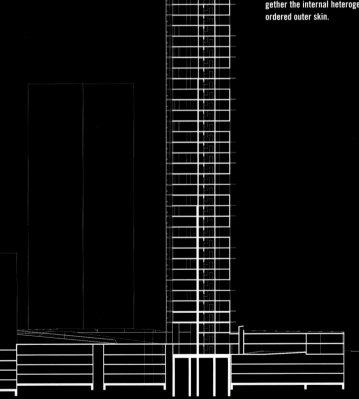

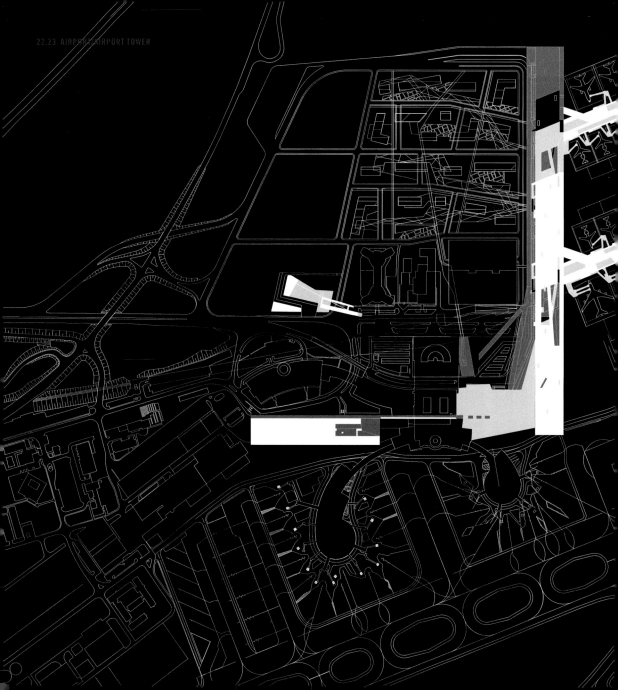

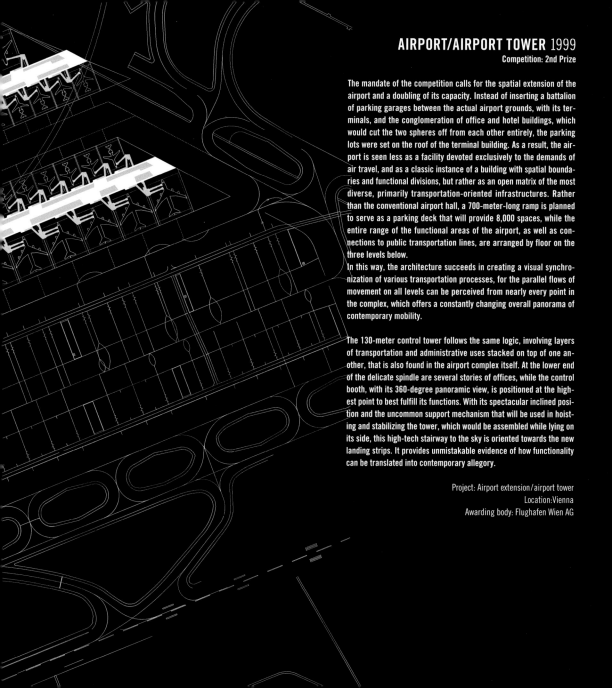

AIRPORT/AIRPORT TOWER 1999
Competition: 2nd Prize

The mandate of the competition calls for the spatial extension of the airport and a doubling of its capacity. Instead of inserting a battalion of parking garages between the actual airport grounds, with its terminals, and the conglomeration of office and hotel buildings, which would cut the two spheres off from each other entirely, the parking lots were set on the roof of the terminal building. As a result, the airport is seen less as a facility devoted exclusively to the demands of air travel, and as a classic instance of a building with spatial boundaries and functional divisions, but rather as an open matrix of the most diverse, primarily transportation-oriented infrastructures. Rather than the conventional airport hall, a 700-meter-long ramp is planned to serve as a parking deck that will provide 8,000 spaces, while the entire range of the functional areas of the airport, as well as connections to public transportation lines, are arranged by floor on the three levels below.

In this way, the architecture succeeds in creating a visual synchronization of various transportation processes, for the parallel flows of movement on all levels can be perceived from nearly every point in the complex, which offers a constantly changing overall panorama of contemporary mobility.

The 130-meter control tower follows the same logic, involving layers of transportation and administrative uses stacked on top of one another, that is also found in the airport complex itself. At the lower end of the delicate spindle are several stories of offices, while the control booth, with its 360-degree panoramic view, is positioned at the highest point to best fulfill its functions. With its spectacular inclined position and the uncommon support mechanism that will be used in hoisting and stabilizing the tower, which would be assembled while lying on its side, this high-tech stairway to the sky is oriented towards the new landing strips. It provides unmistakable evidence of how functionality can be translated into contemporary allegory.

Project: Airport extension / airport tower
Location: Vienna
Awarding body: Flughafen Wien AG

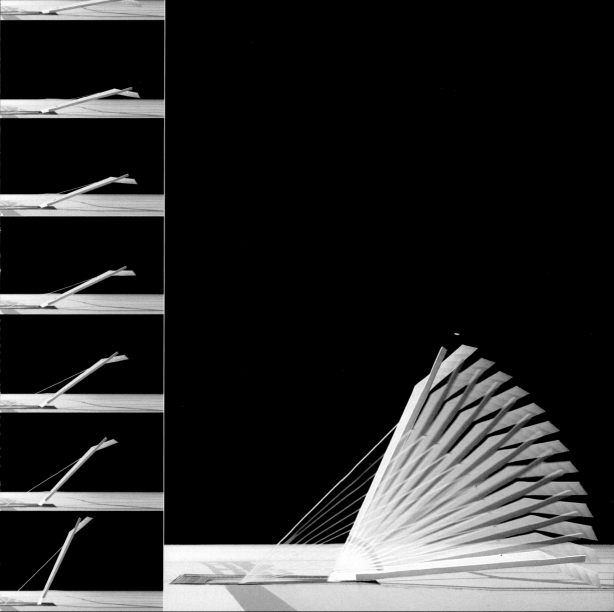

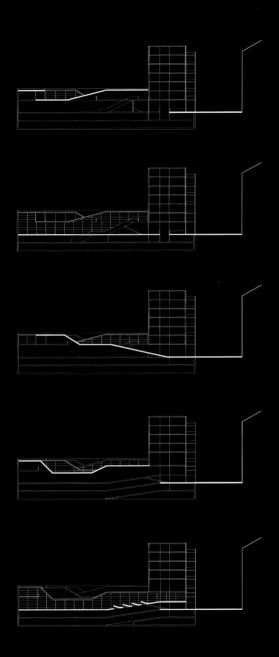

TOWNHOUSE WIMBERGERGASSE 2002

The Wimbergergasse Townhouse occupies a building gap that arose in the dense urban grid of Gründerzeit buildings. Despite its compactness as a part of a classical block development, the complex has an open, permeable character and is communicative, both in respect to the dialogue between the two wings, and the relation between old and new.

The design displays two dominant design motifs – the accentuation of topography and the space-containing feature of the façade – that are merged fluidly both formally and functionally: in the horizontal plane to the rear of the complex, office zones are arranged on two to three levels, flat, like ice floes stacked on top of one other, while vertically it is not the street-side façade of the residential wing that forms the outermost boundary, but instead a modular system of loggias and open spaces which extends beyond it, and which is accentuated into a strong visual impulse.

Number of apartments: 43
Number of offices: 11
Floor area: 5,700 m^2
Site area: 2,900 m^2
Built-up area: 2,600 m^2
Costs/m^2: € 1,271.80

Project: Kallco Project 7.14
Residential and Office Building
Location: Vienna
Client: Kallco Bauträger GmbH, Vienna

32.33 PORSCHE MUSEUM

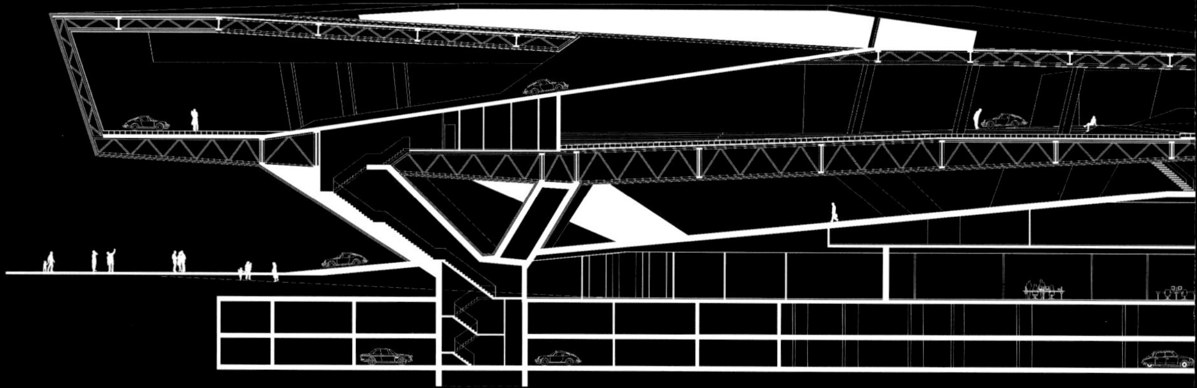

The new Porsche Museum will express the company's self-confide
stance and high standards in architectural terms, while at the sar
time conveying the firm's dynamism and vitality.

The Porsche Museum was conceived as a gravity-defying, dynamica
formed monolithic structure that seems to hover above the fold
topography of the ground and the first-floor levels. It contains t
exhibition area, and provides an opportunity to spatially experien
the Porsche "cosmos".

On the first floor is the entrance area, which acts not only as a foy
and hub but also offering interesting insights into the "roots of tl
Porsche experience," providing visitors with focused views of the vi
tage car workshop and the archive.

The exhibition space is conceived as a vast arena that renounces h
erarchical principles of order and a linear, predetermined single a
proach of presentation. Cross references emerge and can be followe
both spatially and thematically.

Exhibition area: 5,000 r
Restaurants/café: 500 r
Museum shop: 200 r
Classic car workshop: 1,000 r
Conference area: 700 r

Location: Stuttg
Completion: 20
Client: Porsche AG, Stuttga

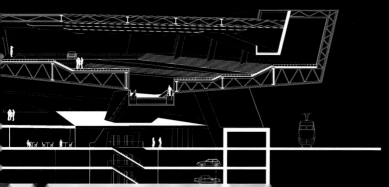

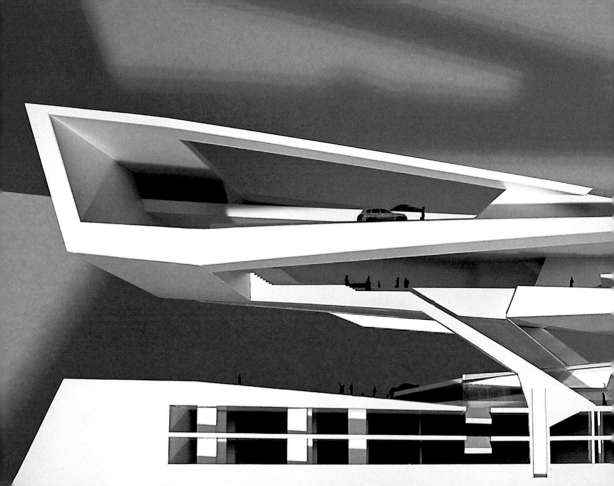

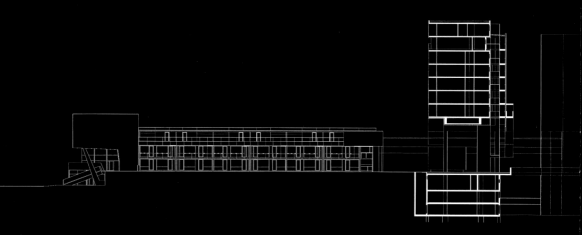

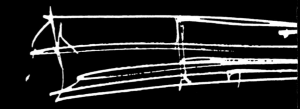

The laconic form of the "Beam" as "horizontal high rise" and the highly visible location of this apartment complex signal, at first glance, both its integration into a larger overall concept and its individualistic conception. This recumbent apartment building follows the shoreline of the New Danube along its entire 180-meter length. Supported by pilotis, the seven-story building is raised like a stage above the plateau-like slab base. With its riverside apartments, the "Beam" offers inhabitants a truly spectacular, contemporary Viennese veduta that stretches from the bars directly below its loggias to the silhouette of the first district in the distance.

From the outer edge to the center of the building, the pilotis vary in height between ten, seven, and four meters, creating spaces of varying size beneath the structure forming a transitional zone. This opening affords not only a spatial visibility for the buildings behind it, but also ensures that this bastion of the private realm is regularly washed by the overlap and fringe of the public sphere. The 190 apartments extend from front to back and have both glazed loggias and glass vestibules that form a part of the network of walkways which lead to the apartments along the glazed rear of the building.

In keeping with the given urban planning situation, but also with contemporary living habits, this building is not a mere "living apparatus," but rather an open container for urban living that offers ample space for diverse lifestyles and can be enjoyed in a frank, hedonistic way.

Number of apartments: 190
Floor area: 20,442 m^2
Built-up area: 3,065 m^2
Costs/m^2: € 1,293.86

Project: Residential Building
Location: Vienna
Client: Donaucity Wohnbau AG, Vienna

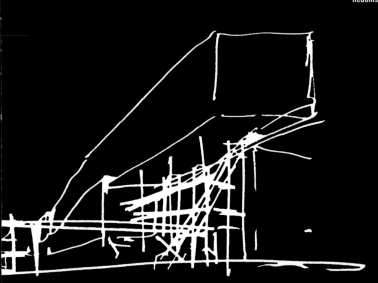

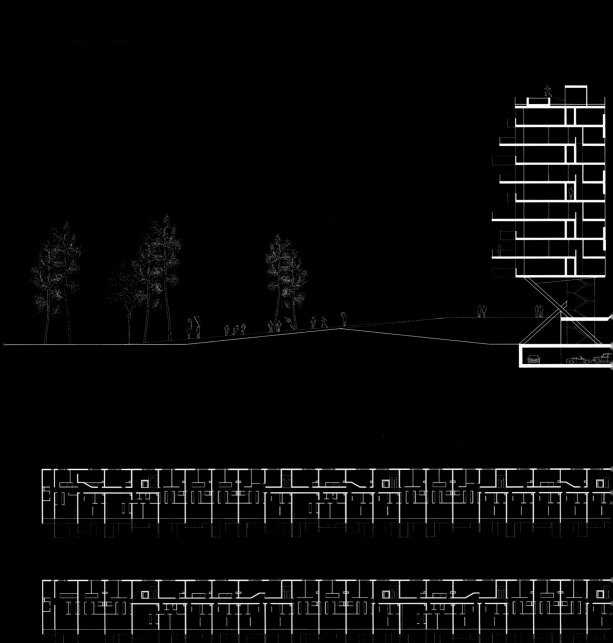

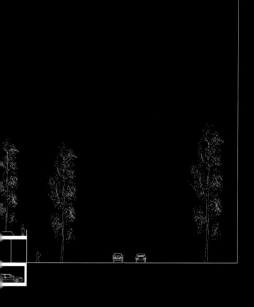

The building volume occupies the border zone between the street area and the vast park grounds, and yet does not define the divide as an impermeable limit, but rather as a place where public, semi-public, and private areas intermingle. Because this 36-meter-high building was set back from the street line, it was permitted to surpass the height stipulated in the original competition brief. At the same time, this expansion of the street area corresponds to the scale of the park, which extends beneath the raised structure. As a topographical element, the base of the building serves as a link between urban and natural realms.

The street-side façade was conceived as a flat surface, while the side facing the park bears a three-dimensional fractal structure: in addition to the sheltered loggias, deeply cantilevered balconies allow a conscious step outward into the park. As an extension of the park's leisure facilities, the roof offers residents access to a pool, sauna, and terrace with a panoramic view.

The circulation zones are a modification of a central corridor type: they consist of several short, compact, naturally lit passageways that lead both to the apartments as well as to the offices located on the street-side of the building – individually rentable workspaces which optionally extend the apartments.

Number of apartments: 204
Building length: 192 m
Gross floor space: 27,000 m^2

Project: Residential Building
Location: Vienna
Awarding body: GESIBA, Vienna
City of Vienna MA 21A

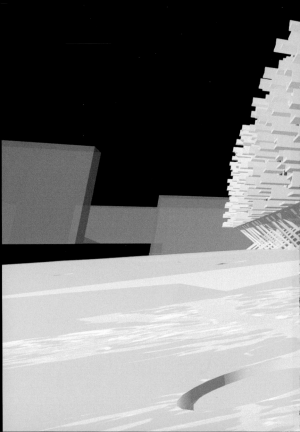

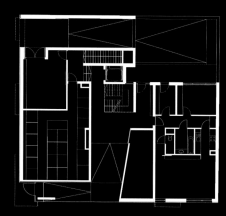

Grundriss EG

Grundriss 5 . OG

APARTMENTS PALTRAMPLATZ 2002

This residential building leaves an indelible mark on the densely packed landscape of Gründerzeit buildings, amidst which it stands out as a sharply delineated, monolithic, matte black cube whose jutting, irregularly arranged, bright loggias charge the entire structure by introducing an element of contrast .

These floor-to-ceiling glazed loggias, which interact with the elegant mosaic of freely-arranged, dark Eternit slabs, function as extensions of the apartments into the green space of the park, at the same time serving as the central element determining the appearance of the façade.

The extremely cantilevered, perforated roof construction, provides a counterweight to the severity of this corner building and caps its upper edge with a dynamic gesture. The rooftop terrace is open to all, and its sauna and relaxation zones offer attractive places of rest for all residents. Embedded in the roof are photovoltaic cells that can store enough energy to fuel the facilities in the common access zones.

Through a clever interplay of various constellations of spatial modules, the building is reminiscent of the legendary Rubik's Cube, a toy popular in the 1980s that challenged the coordination and intelligence of an entire generation.

Number of apartments: 22
Floor area: 1,550 m^2
Site area: 387 m^2
Costs/m^2: € 1,100.00

Project: Residential Building
Location: Vienna
Client: Neues Leben, Vienna

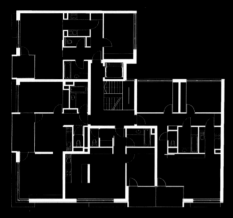

Grundriss 2 . OG

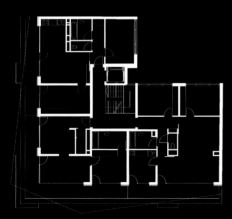

Grundriss Dachgeschoss

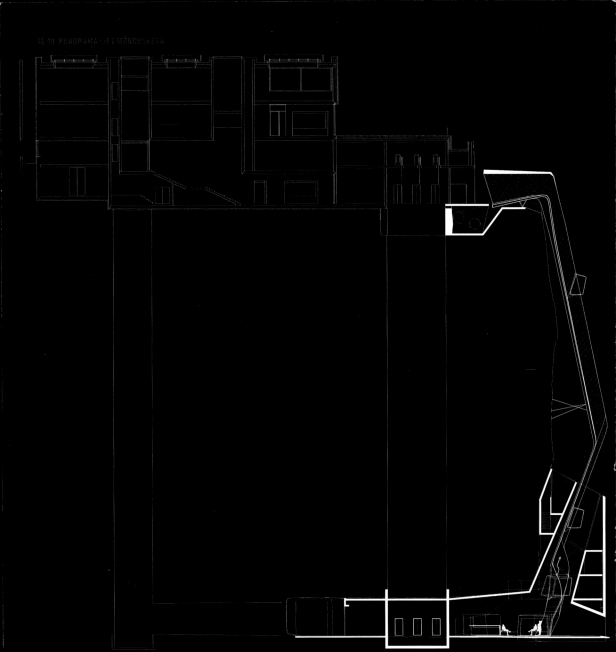

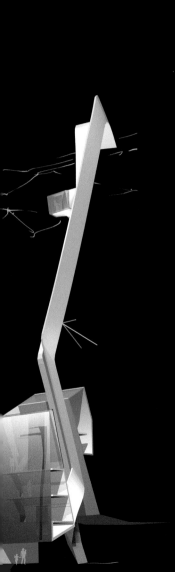

With the aim of developing an important symbol for this site and be
yond, this plan proposes a reinterpretation of the classic lift theme.
As an access to the museum, this panorama lift goes far beyond ful
filling merely functional demands. Indeed, the spectacular journey up
the steep rock face of the Mönchsberg itself becomes a multi-percep
tional experience. The lift does not simply follow the shortest route
from point A to point B, but instead traces out a path derived from
the characteristic topography of the Mönchsberg. The amorphous
form of the track which conducts the cabin visualizes the trajectory
of the cabin as it might be recorded by time-lapse photography, and
its manifestation as an architectonic symbol in conjunction with the
rock face of the Mönchsberg.
In order to allow the entrance to take advantage of the width of the
space and to ensure a visual link to existing internal elevators, the
entry and exit position of the cabin of the panorama lift is positioned
lengthwise and off to one side. Since the cabin does not begin its 90
rotation until after the cabin has begun its ascent, it is possible to
make full use of both the longer, panoramic window side of the cabin
and the floor plan of the lower station. Still within the building, the
cabin stages itself as a spatial event as it twists upward, breaking out
into the open in an interplay of narrow confines and vast expanse.

Height: 60 m
Cabin capacity: 20-25 person
Floor area (foyer): 54 m

Location: Salzburg
Awarding body: Salzburg AG

092007

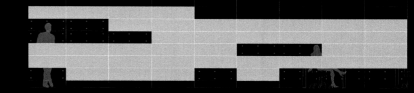

The flexible NovaMobile shelf system was developed especially for N
vartis. Its basic function is to separate passageways and office spa
es while simultaneously forming zones of differing densities that d
pend upon the requirements and communication values of each giv
place. The combination of different module types (shelf systems, ca
inets with or without doors) mounted on floor-to-ceiling, load-beari
glass walls enables the formation of hermetic, semitransparent,
well as transparent zones. This is achieved through variable assembl
options which make it possible to take into consideration the spont
neous on-site preferences of individual employees. At the same tim
NovaMobile serves as a space-defining element and visual guideli
throughout the entire spatial context. Through the interplay of t
graphical linearity of the module system and the backlit screen p
sitioned vis-à-vis, the hallway area becomes a dynamic space who
impact emphasizes the vastness of the spatial impression while goi
beyond the functional aspect.

Costs/m^2: € 645.
Costs/shelf module: € 1,400.0
Floor area: 2,900

Project: Global Headquarters Sando
Novartis Company, Interior Desi
Location: Vien
Client: BC Biochemie Pharma GmbH, Ismani

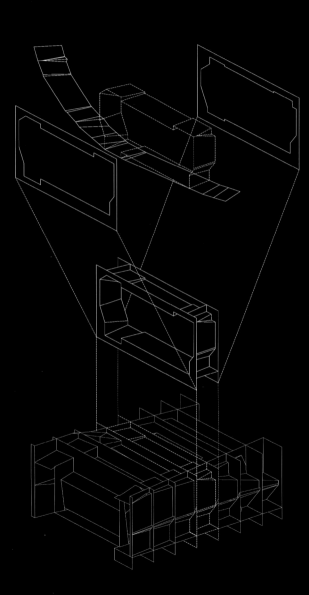

DEEP SURFACE 2004

In light of China's rapidly growing architectural development, it seems obvious to lend spatial expression to the fast pace and dynamism of these processes. The uninterrupted change to which Beijing's cityscape is constantly subjected has taken on an almost virtual character, one that nevertheless also adheres to the reality of the construction industry. The contrast between such seemingly irreconcilable concepts as speed and contemplation or virtuality and reality forms the basis of this design.

The apartment is conceived as a flowing spatial continuum. This is achieved via a multiply convoluted crystalline "furniture landscape" which consistently recognizes floors, ceiling, and walls as equal parameters. The given spatial layout is undermined, though not actually negated, by this "architecture of transition," while the classical linear spatial boundaries expand, unfolding themselves and becoming perceptible as great convolutions. Converging here is the tensely stark contrast of an architecture that on the one hand possesses a strong spatial presence in its expressiveness and dynamism, while on the other appearing as an unobtrusive, diffusely-lit spatial configuration that must first be discovered, felt and experienced by the observer.

Floor area: 150 m^2

Project: Apartment Unit 8-II, Phoenix City
Exhibition: 1st Architectural Biennial Beijing
A5 Infinite Interior
Location: Beijing
Client: CR Land China Resources, Beijing

AGENZIA SPAZIALE ITALIANA 2000
Competition

As the research and administration center of the Italian Space Agency, the Agenzia Spaziale Italiana deals with mobility at the speed of
light and organizes exhibitions and events for the general public.
The mandate of the competition, therefore, calls for a building that,
embedded in the center of ancient Rome and flanked by prominent
contemporary architecture, will guarantee maximum security and
discretion, at the same time serving as an attractive public symbol.
These requirements, focused on functionally and topography, were
approached with an "invisible" design that places the complex almost
entirely beneath the surface of the urban threshold of perception, and
only reveals its spectacular nature upon closer inspection.

Height: -25 m
Site area: 4,018 m^2

Project: Italian Space Agency
Location: Rome
Awarding body: Agenzia Spaziale Italiana

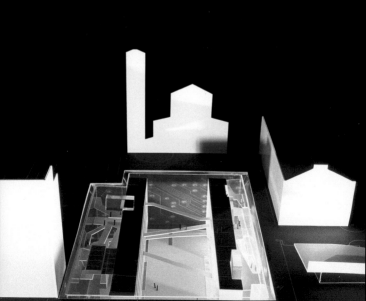

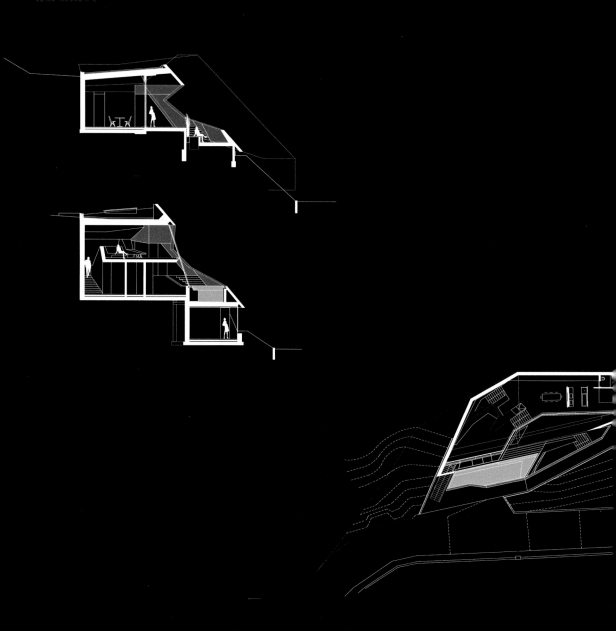

HOUSE H-L 2007

The extreme hillside situation of the designated property serves as the key design parameter and is also a space-defining feature of the building structure. The single-family house inserts itself deep into the slope, which thus also becomes the living space, and leaves only the striking streetside façade exposed to public view. A frame, encircling the front of the building like a shield, protectively hides the internal functions, which extend at varying levels into the hillside. This frame also incorporates outdoor areas located in front of the house, such as the swimming pool and terraces. The internal path through the building traces the extreme slope of the property over the various levels and plateaus. The natural environment thus becomes a ubiquitously perceptible aspect of living, and the internal path takes the exposed situation into consideration with a sweeping view of the hinterland on the fringe of urban Vienna.

Site area: 578 m^2
Built-up area: 148 m^2
Usable floor space: 263 m^2

Project: Single Family Home
Location: Vienna
Completion: 2007
Client: Private

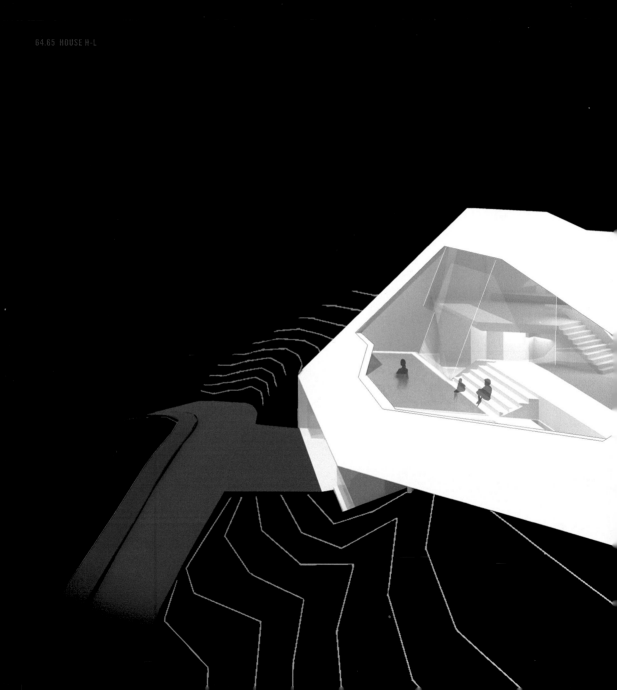

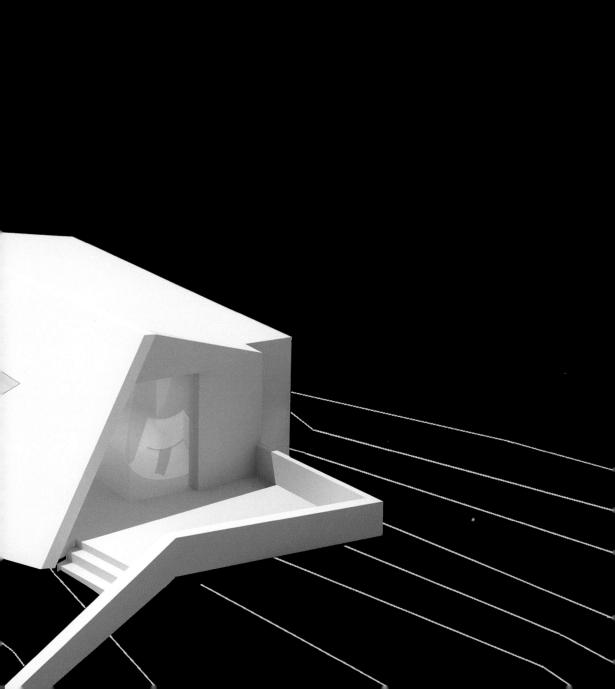

66.67 HOUSE OEDBERG

HOUSE OEDBERG 2005
Competition

House Oedberg was conceived for a northern slope and is thus oriented both formally and functionally toward the south, where the expansive landscape is characterized strongly by the vineyards and woods. The living area on the first floor follows the differences in levels of the existing site topography. Loft-like open spaces dominate here, and dispense with visual partitions; introverted bedrooms on the second floor provide possibilities for discreet withdrawal.

The building's "spine", which rises from the topography with its front side as a raised, wide-open gesture, determines the building's outward appearance as an idiosyncratically shaped sculpture. In order to emphasize the elevated position of the house, the access route at the foot of the hill, where the garage is also located, is staged as a passageway that cuts deep into the slope, providing a spectacular entrance experience, reemerging inside the house where it unfolds into the open living area.

Usable floor space: 412 m^2
Site area: 1300 m^2
Built-up area: 220 m^2

Project: Single Family Home
Location: Vienna
Awarding body: Private

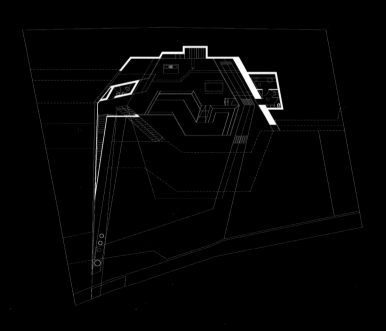

The famous three stripe logo is much more than simply an internationally recognized trademark. It also represent the particular attitude that propels adidas, and which makes it distinctive in every regard. The Adi Dassler Brand Center constitutes the heart of the "World of Sports" in Bad Herzogenaurach. The design takes into consideration the specific topological and contextual situation, with the aim of positioning the building optimally vis-à-vis internal and external functions, while taking full advantage of its qualities of its rapport with the surrounding environment, as well as existing or projected architecture in the vicinity.

Primarily through the visitors' experience of its functions and through the spatial and sensory stimuli it provides, this building embodies qualities that are intrinsic to adidas: speed, concentration, power, coolness, generosity, and self-confidence.

Gross floor space: 12,842 m^2
Site area: 1.6 ha

Location: Herzogenaurach
Awarding body: Adidas Salomon AG

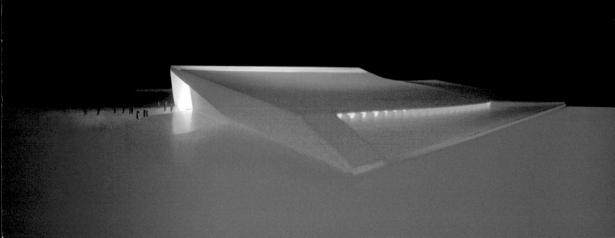

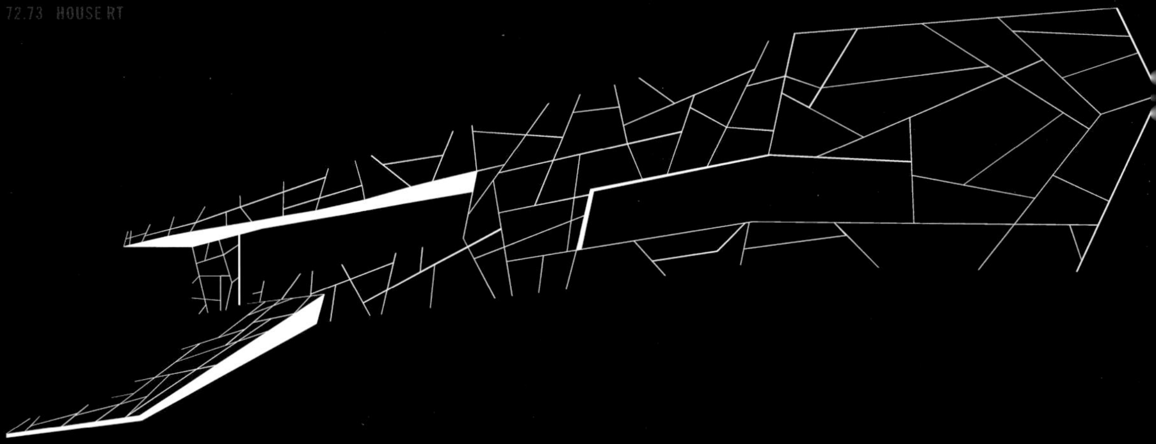

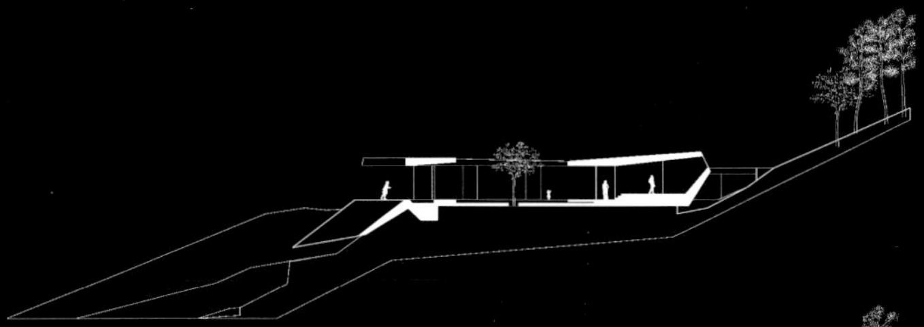

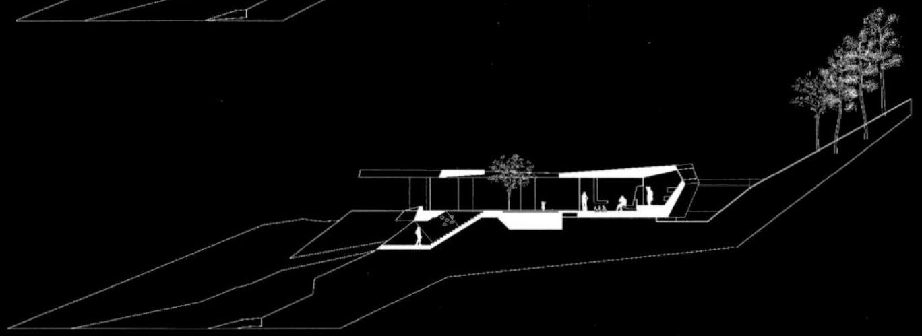

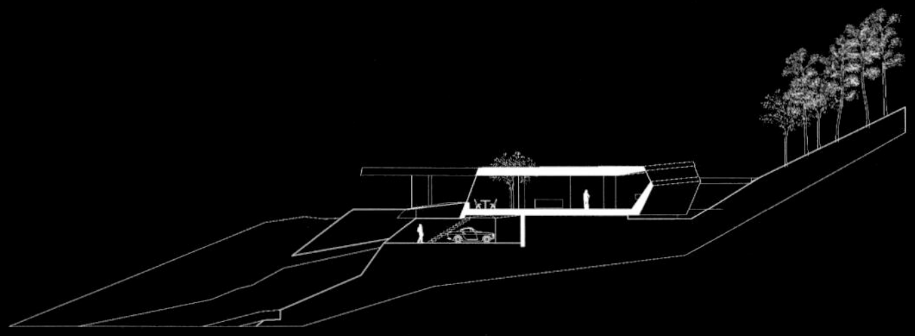

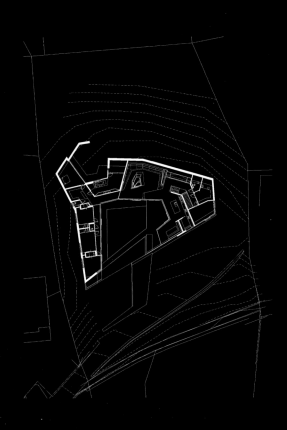

HOUSE RT 2005

The sloping terrain at the edge of the woods presents an impressive panoramic view of the valley and the surrounding mountain landscape. The imposing and highly specific topography of the site is the design's point of departure: the house is placed at the center of a clearing and conceived as an atrium structure. The atrium reflects the specific appearance of this environment while at the same time organizing a visual and spatial relation with the internal structure.

This offers the inhabitants defined yet open options for retreat, as well as spectacular sweeping views and ideal opportunities for spending time outdoors.

The building incorporates itself cautiously into its surroundings, to some extent interpreting the parameters of the terrain architecturally. Through its sculptural form and the black crack pattern of the façade the house positions itself boldly in the charged interaction with nature – whether buried beneath a blanket of snow or marked by lush green.

Site area: 2791 m^2
Usable floor space: 554 m^2
Built-up area: 668 m^2

Project: Single Family Home
Location: Austria
Client: Private

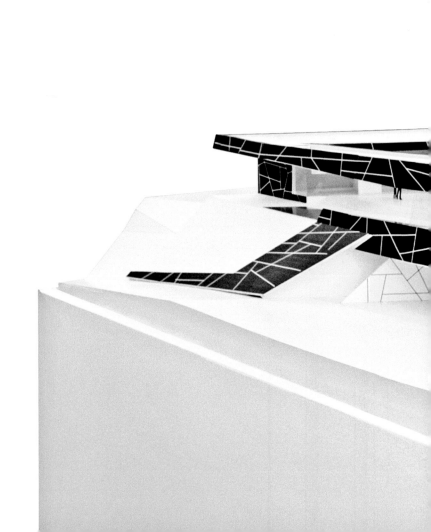

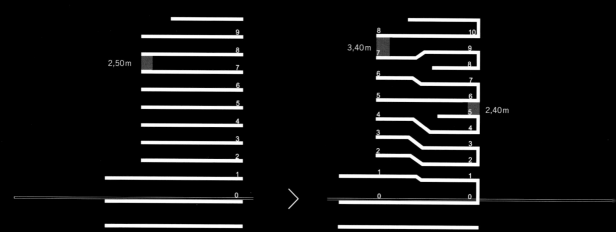

KALLCO CITY LOFTS WIENERBERG 2004

The project forms one component of a large new urban development in Wienerberg, Vienna. The scheme for a site on the west side of this area incorporates living and working spaces within an eleven-story building on a footprint measuring 44 by 22 meters.

In place of the simple stacking of identical layers, the design uses interlocking floors to create spaces of differing heights. The result is an interlaced wickerwork of levels so complex that eight cross sections are required to explain the structure. Despite a nominal room height of 2.5 meters, this configuration allows lofty living areas of 3.4 meters to the south as well as lower zones of 2.4 meters to the north, designed for sleep and recreation. The differentiated floor heights are of primary importance for the economic feasibility of the project, for this innovative design results in an additional story on the north side of the building.

This design permits a multiplicity of dwelling types from bachelor pads to split-level apartments, with glazed office units and studios on the north side. The complex interplay of domestic and working spaces is revealed in the dynamic north façade. By contrast, a continuous ribbon of balconies with balustrades screens the apartments on the south side.

Number of apartments: 47
Floor area: 5,313 m^2
Built-up area: 968 m^2
Costs/m^2: € 1,152.00

Project: Residential Building with Offices and a Kindergarten
Location: Vienna
Client: Kallco Bauträger GmbH, Vienna

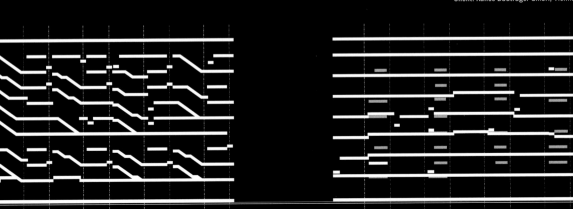

FILMMUSEUM 2009

Competition: 1st Prize

Conceived as a free-standing sculpture on an eye-catching site, the planned Filmmuseum in Amsterdam has yet to find its equal in kind and dimensions anywhere in the world. It positions itself vis-à-vis the old part of the city and the Central Station on the shoreline of the IJ River. The Filmmuseum is designed as a dynamic entity. Even from afar, the appearance of its crystalline geometry changes perpetually in the shifting play of light. To approach the Filmmuseum from the city center is to experience a "dramaturgy" of differing spatial and visual sequences. Architecturally, the Filmmuseum addresses the parameters of motion and light that are especially thematically relevant to the medium of film. These become elements that endow the building with a unique identity while enhancing the perception and experience of it on this unique site.

The sweeping central "arena" serves as the Filmmuseum's spatial and functional focal point, and serves as an interface between exterior space and various internal uses. It thereby acts simultaneously as light-infused rendezvous point, stage, relaxation zone, point of departure and arrival, vista platform, bar, café, restaurant, and living area.

Floor area: 5,700 m^2

Gross floor space: 8,200 m^2

Theaters: 1 x 80, 2 x 120, 1 x 300 seats

Exhibition area: 1,100 m^2

Office area: 1,200 m^2

Information center: 500 m^2 incl. collection, study room, study booths, public PC workstations

Restaurant/bar/café: 400 m^2

Location: Amsterdam

Completion: 2009

Project development: ING Real Estate

Client: Filmmuseum Amsterdam